Hip
HIMALAYANS

FLUFFY! REGAL! LOVING!

SOCIAL! GENTLE! SWEET!

ABDO
Publishing Company

Katherine Hengel

Consulting Editor, Diane Craig, M.A./Reading Specialist

Published by ABDO Publishing Company
8000 West 78th Street, Edina, Minnesota 55439.

Printed in the United States.

 PRINTED ON RECYCLED PAPER

Editor: Liz Salzmann
Content Developer: Nancy Tuminelly
Cover and Interior Design and Production:
   Anders Hanson, Mighty Media
Illustrations: Bob Doucet
Photo Credits: Chanan (p.4–7), Shutterstock

Library of Congress Cataloging-in-Publication Data
Hengel, Katherine.
 Hip himalayans / Katherine Hengel ; illustrations by Bob
Doucet.
   p. cm. -- (Cat craze)
 ISBN 978-1-60453-722-2
 1. Himalayan cat--Juvenile literature. I. Doucet, Bob, ill. II.
Title.

 SF449.H55H46 2010
 636.8'3--dc22
                    2009004031

Super SandCastle™ books are created by a team of
professional educators, reading specialists, and content
developers around five essential components—phonemic
awareness, phonics, vocabulary, text comprehension, and
fluency—to assist young readers as they develop reading
skills and strategies and increase their general
knowledge. All books are written, reviewed, and leveled
for guided reading, early reading intervention, and
Accelerated Reader® programs for use in shared, guided,
and independent reading and writing activities to support
a balanced approach to literacy instruction.

CONTENTS

The
HIMALAYAN

Himalayans are beautiful cats with long, fluffy coats. Their coats are mostly white or cream colored. They have darker fur on their faces, ears, legs, feet, and tails. Himalayans are sweet, cuddly, and very social. Himalayans are sometimes called Himmies.

FACIAL FEATURES

Head

Himalayans have wide, round heads that are large compared to their bodies.

Muzzle

A Himalayan can have a flat **muzzle** or a rounded muzzle.

Eyes

Himalayans have large, round eyes that are set far apart. All Himalayans have blue eyes.

Ears

Their ears are small with rounded tips. They are set low on the cat's head.

BODY BASICS

Size
Adult Himalayans weigh about 12 to 15 pounds (5 to 7 kg).

Build
Himalayans have broad, round bodies. They are heavy-boned cats.

Tail
Their tails don't curve very much. Himalayans don't often raise their tails higher than their backs.

Legs and Feet
Himalayans have short legs and large, round feet.

COAT & COLOR

SEAL FUR

CHOCOLATE FUR

BLUE FUR

Himalayan Fur

Himalayans have long, fluffy fur. They may feel uncomfortable in hot weather because their coats are so thick. The coat is mostly a light color such as white or cream. The fur on the face, ears, legs, feet, and tail is darker. These darker areas are called points. The points come in several colors and patterns. Some Himalayans have very light points that are hard to see.

BLUE POINT

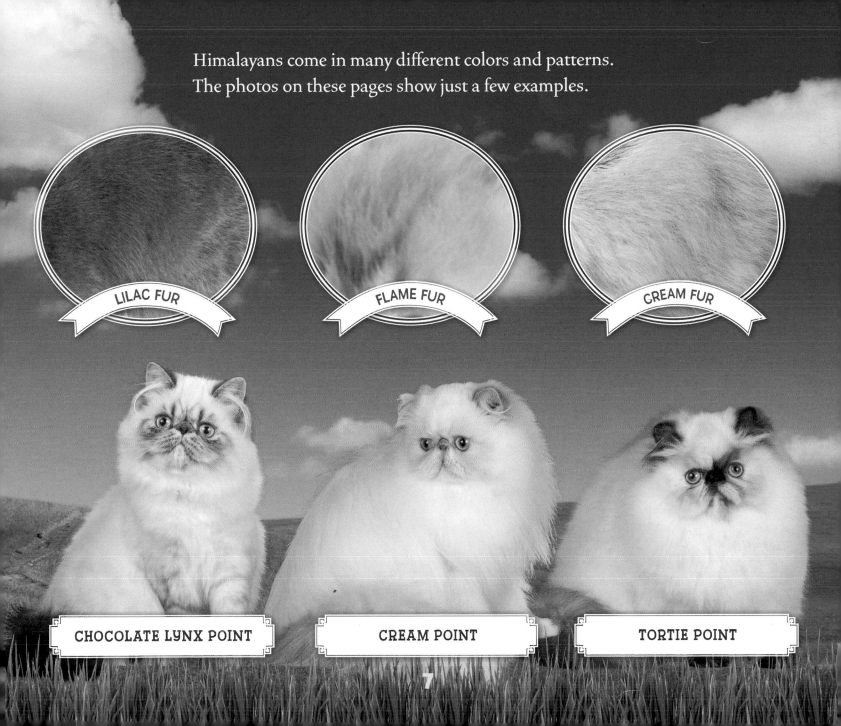

Himalayans come in many different colors and patterns.
The photos on these pages show just a few examples.

LILAC FUR

FLAME FUR

CREAM FUR

CHOCOLATE LYNX POINT

CREAM POINT

TORTIE POINT

7

HEALTH & CARE

Life Span

Himalayans can live for 15 years or more!

Health Concerns

Himalayans need to be brushed once a day. If they aren't, they will get tangles and **hairballs**. Their eyes often get watery. It is important to clean them every day. Himalayans with flat **muzzles** can have trouble breathing.

VET'S CHECKLIST

- Have your Himalayan spayed or neutered. This will prevent unwanted kittens.

- Visit a vet for regular checkups.

- Don't let your Himalayan get too hot.

- Clean your Himalayan's teeth and ears once a week.

- Brush your Himalayan and clean its eyes once a day.

- Ask your vet about shots that may benefit your cat.

ATTITUDE & BEHAVIOR

Personality

Himalayans like to be close to their owners. They love attention, and they like to be **groomed**. They are gentle and sweet.

Activity Level

Himalayans are relaxed and calm. They love to sit on laps! But they like to play too. Some Himalayans even play fetch with their owners!

All About Me

Hi! My name is Horatio. I'm a Himalayan. I just wanted to let you know a few things about me. I made some lists below of things I like and dislike. Check them out!

Things I Like

- Hanging out inside
- Having my long coat brushed
- Being picked up or cuddled
- Sitting on my owner's lap
- Playing with toys
- Following my owner around the house
- Taking naps

Things I Dislike

- Getting dirty
- Having a lot of tears around my eyes
- Being alone for long periods of time
- Being in the middle of a lot of activity
- Being in really hot places

LITTERS & KITTENS

Litter Size

Female Himalayans usually give birth to three to six kittens.

Diet

Newborn kittens drink their mother's milk. They can begin to eat kitten food when they are about 4 weeks old. Kitten food is different from cat food. It has extra **protein**, fat, and **vitamins** that help kittens grow.

Growth

Himalayan kittens should stay with their mothers for at least 12 weeks.
A Himalayan will be almost full grown when it is six months old.
But it will continue to grow slowly until it is one year old.

BUYING A HIMALAYAN

Choosing a Breeder

It's best to buy a kitten from a **breeder**, not a pet store. When you visit a cat breeder, ask to see the mother and father of the kittens. Make sure the parents are healthy, friendly, and well **behaved**.

Picking a Kitten

Choose a kitten that isn't too active or too shy. If you sit down, some of the kittens may come over to you. One of them might be the right one for you!

Is It the Right Cat for You?

Buying a cat is a big decision. You'll want to make sure your new pet suits your lifestyle.

Get out a piece of paper. Draw a line down the middle.

Read the statements listed here. Each time you agree with a statement from the left column, make a mark on the left side of your paper. When you agree with a statement from the right column, make a mark on the right side of your paper.

I want a cat that likes to cuddle.	☐	☐	I don't want a cat that needs lots of attention.
It's fun to groom an animal with long fur!	☐	☐	I don't want to brush my cat's fur very often.
Cats that like to take naps are great!	☐	☐	I would like a very active cat.
I want a cat that is content inside.	☐	☐	I want a cat that likes to spend time outside.
I don't mind wiping my cat's eyes.	☐	☐	I don't want to clean my cat's eyes.

If you made more marks on the left side than on the right side, a Himalayan may be the right cat for you! If you made more marks on the right side of your paper, you might want to consider another breed.

Some Things You'll Need

Cats go to the bathroom in a **litter box**. It should be kept in a quiet place. Most cats learn to use their litter box all by themselves. You just have to show them where it is! The dirty **litter** should be scooped out every day. The litter should be changed completely every week.

Your cat's **food and water dishes** should be wide and shallow. This helps your cat keep its whiskers clean. The dishes should be in a different area than the litter box. Cats do not like to eat and go to the bathroom in the same area.

Cats love to scratch! **Scratching posts** help keep cats from scratching the furniture. The scratching post should be taller than your cat. It should have a wide, heavy base so it won't tip over.

Cats are natural predators. Without small animals to hunt, cats may become bored and unhappy. **Cat toys** can satisfy your cat's need to chase and capture. They will help keep your cat entertained and happy.

Cats should not play with balls of yarn or string. If they accidentally eat the yarn, they could get sick.

Cat claws should be trimmed regularly with special cat claw **clippers**. Regular nail clippers will also work. Some people choose to have their cat's claws removed by a vet. But most vets and animal rights groups think declawing is cruel.

You should comb your cat regularly with a **cat hair comb**. This will help keep its coat healthy and clean.

A **cat bed** will give your cat a safe, comfortable place to sleep.

LIVING WITH A HIMALAYAN

Being a Good Companion

Himalayans need a lot of attention. To prevent tangles, you should brush your Himalayan every day. Many owners bathe their Himalayans too.

Inside or Outside?

Himalayans should be kept inside. If they go outside, dirt and leaves will get in their long fur. Satisfy their need for adventure with plenty of playtime and toys! Also, Himalayans need to be in air-conditioned homes in hot weather. Remember, they have thick coats on all year round!

Feeding Your Himalayan

Feed your Himalayan wet or dry cat food. Your vet can help you choose the best food for your cat.

Cleaning the Litter Box

Like all cats, Himalayans are tidy. They don't like smelly or dirty litter boxes. If the litter box is dirty, they may go to the bathroom somewhere else. Ask your vet for advice if your cat isn't using its box.

☠ DANGER: POISONOUS FOODS

Some people like to feed their cats table scraps. Here are some human foods that can make cats sick.

TOMATOES

POTATOES

ONIONS

GARLIC

CHOCOLATE

GRAPES

THE PERFECT MIX

In the 1930s, Dr. Clyde Keller and Virginia Cobb created a new kind of cat. They wanted a cat with a long coat like a Persian cat. They also wanted it to have color points like a Siamese. So they **bred** Siamese with Persian cats! Several years later, the first Himalayan cat was born.

In England, Himalayans are called Colourpoint Persians or Longhaired Colourpoints. In 1955, the Governing Council of the Cat Fancy made the Colourpoint Persian an official **breed**. Other groups consider the Himalayan to be a type of Persian.

#1

FIND THE
HIMALAYAN

A

B

C

D

THE HIMALAYAN QUIZ

1. Himalayans are sometimes called Himmies. **True or false?**

2. Himalayans have short fur. **True or false?**

3. All Himalayans are the same color. **True or false?**

4. Himalayans love attention. **True or false?**

5. Himalayans should be kept outdoors. **True or false?**

6. In England, Himalayans are called Colourpoint Persians. **True or false?**

GLOSSARY

behave - to act in a certain way.

breed - 1) a group of animals or plants with common ancestors. 2) to raise animals that have certain traits. A *breeder* is someone whose job is to breed certain animals or plants.

groom - to clean the fur of an animal.

hairball - fur that has formed a clump in a cat's stomach. It can cause the cat to throw up.

muzzle - an animal's nose and jaws.

protein - a substance found in all plant and animal cells.

vitamin - a substance needed for good health, found naturally in plants and meats.

About SUPER SANDCASTLE™

Bigger Books for Emerging Readers
Grades K–4

Created for library, classroom, and at-home use, Super SandCastle™ books support and engage young readers as they develop and build literacy skills and will increase their general knowledge about the world around them. Super SandCastle™ books are part of SandCastle™, the leading preK–3 imprint for emerging and beginning readers. Super SandCastle™ features a larger trim size for more reading fun.

Let Us Know

Super SandCastle™ would like to hear your stories about reading this book. What was your favorite page? Was there something hard that you needed help with? Share the ups and downs of learning to read. We want to hear from you! Send us an e-mail.

sandcastle@abdopublishing.com

Contact us for a complete list of SandCastle™, Super SandCastle™, and other nonfiction and fiction titles from ABDO Publishing Company.

www.abdopublishing.com • 8000 West 78th Street Edina, MN 55439 • 800-800-1312 • 952-831-1632 fax